LIFE IN THE RECENT PAST

Lisa looks b[ack]

Rhonda Glasgow & Sheila Tinsley

Illustrations by
Bill Walsh

Contents

This is Lisa, who is eight years old.
She has a dog called Sammy and
a cat called Fudge.

**Granny was born
in 1933**

**Mum was
in 19**

1 9 2 0   **1 9 3 0**   **1 9 4 0**   **1 9 5 0**

Lisa's Mum is called Patricia.
She grew up in the country but now
she lives in Belfast with Lisa
and her Dad.

**Lisa was born
in 1986**

1 9 6 0   1 9 7 0   1 9 8 0   1 9 9 0

Lisa's grandparents live on
a small farm in the country.
This is her Granny.

1940s

Granny remembers the war

Lisa was visiting her grandparents at their farm. She was exploring in a shed at the back of their house when she discovered an old box. When she opened it, she found a strange mask. She took it to her Granny to see if she knew what it was for.

Gas mask in its box

Lisa's Granny smiled when she saw it. 'Oh, I remember this so well. Imagine that still being in the shed. I had that when I was about your age. Everyone had to have a gas mask during the war, in case the Germans dropped poisonous gas over the country,' she said.

'It's horrible!' said Lisa. 'Did you really have to wear *that?* Yuk!'

'Well that was the funny thing,' said Granny, 'we had to carry them everywhere for a long time, and we practised using them, but thank goodness, we never needed them.'

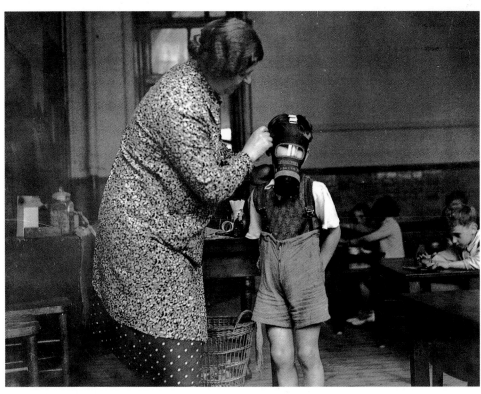

During the Second World War, children were fitted with gas masks at school.

5

'I couldn't be bothered carrying that around everywhere,' said Lisa.

'Oh, you got used to it,' said Granny, 'you just *had* to carry it, you see. Look! My identity card is still in the box, too.'

'What did you need that for?' asked Lisa.

'Everyone, even children, had an identity card to prove you were who you said you were,' replied Granny.

'Why?' asked Lisa.

'Oh, I suppose it was to prove you weren't a spy,' laughed Granny.

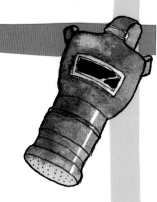

KEY ACTIVITIES

Do you know anyone who remembers the Second World War?
Ask them what age they were then,
and what they remember about wartime.

Why do you think Lisa's grandmother had to carry a gas mask?

What kind of cards can be used today to identify
adults and children and what information would they contain?

Evacuation

Grandad told Lisa what it was like to be an evacuee during the war.

'I was living in Belfast and when the warnings came of bombing raids my Mum and Dad thought that it would be safer for my sister and me to go to stay in the country. We stayed with kind people on their farm in County Fermanagh for three years.'

Children evacuated from Belfast on arrival in County Derry

'At first I hated living in the country,' Grandad said. 'Once I got settled in school it was OK, but my sister and I were very homesick at times. Mum and Dad came to visit us as often as they could and told us what was happening at home. When we went back to live in Belfast I was horrified to see all the damage that had been done.'

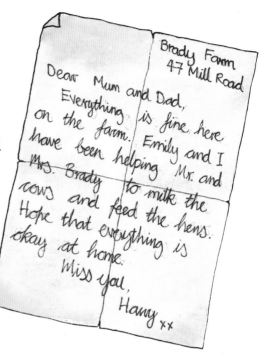

Brady Farm
47 Mill Road

Dear Mum and Dad,
Everything is fine here on the farm. Emily and I have been helping Mr. and Mrs. Brady to milk the cows and feed the hens. Hope that everything is okay at home.
Miss you,
Harry xx

Bomb damage in Belfast after an air raid in 1941

9

The Blitz in Belfast

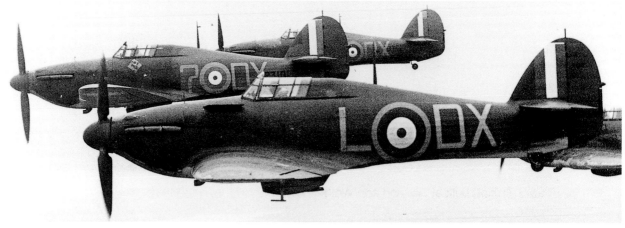

Hurricane fighter planes based in County Down

Lots of weapons were needed to fight the war. The government asked the factories in Belfast to build fighter aircraft and tanks. The famous shipyard Harland and Wolff built warships. The Germans tried to stop this work by attacking Belfast. In 1941 many houses and factories were damaged or destroyed by bombs dropped from German planes and many people were killed and injured. These attacks became known as the Blitz.

Tank assembly line at the munitions factory, Queen's Island, Belfast

HMS *Black Prince*, built at Harland and Wolff

Because so many men were away from home fighting in the war, women were asked to do the work that men usually did in the factories and on the farms. A lot of women were good at this type of work and were sorry to leave their jobs when the war was over.

Women training for factory work at Belfast College of Technology during the Second World War

11

Rationing

Food was very scarce during the war years. To make sure everyone got their fair share, rationing was introduced. Each person in a house got a ration book, with coupons inside it. The coupons allowed each person to buy only a limited amount of food each week.

Each person was only allowed 2 oz (50 g) of sweets or chocolate each week.

Adult weekly food ration

However, not all food was rationed. There was plenty of vegetables, like potatoes, onions and carrots, because people were able to grow these in their gardens, even their front gardens.

Potato Pete

During the war imported fruits, like bananas, were impossible to get, and when they arrived in the shops after the war, children who had never tasted them had a lovely surprise.

13

Food on the farm

During the war Granny's family were more fortunate than families which lived in towns. As well as their rationed food, they had the goods they produced on their farm.

'I helped to make butter from the cream of the milk,' Granny recalled to Lisa. 'We had our own special print to put on the butter. We all loved to melt the butter on hot home-made bread. It was a big favourite. I still make soda bread.'

Here is Granny's recipe for soda bread.

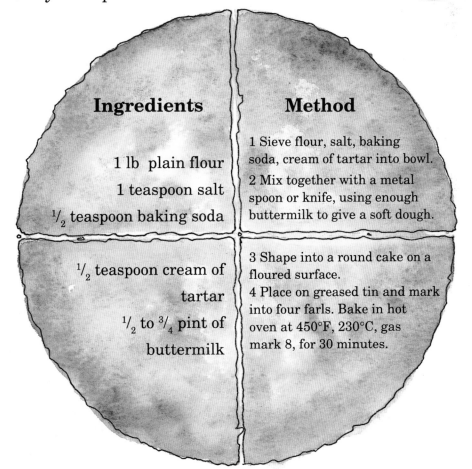

Ingredients

1 lb plain flour

1 teaspoon salt

$\frac{1}{2}$ teaspoon baking soda

$\frac{1}{2}$ teaspoon cream of tartar

$\frac{1}{2}$ to $\frac{3}{4}$ pint of buttermilk

Method

1 Sieve flour, salt, baking soda, cream of tartar into bowl.

2 Mix together with a metal spoon or knife, using enough buttermilk to give a soft dough.

3 Shape into a round cake on a floured surface.

4 Place on greased tin and mark into four farls. Bake in hot oven at 450°F, 230°C, gas mark 8, for 30 minutes.

War posters like these told people
to be careful and not to waste anything,
and to work hard to defeat the enemy.

KEY ACTIVITIES

★

Keep a diary for a week to record how much food you eat each day at
breakfast time, lunch time, tea time and supper time.
Don't forget snacks and sweets.
Compare your record with the amount of food illustrated on page 12.
What do you think might have happened if there
had not been rationing?

★

Using the illustration on page 14, describe how Granny's family
produced their own food during the time of rationing.

★

Look at the posters on pages 13 and 16. Make your own
wartime poster to encourage people to grow their own food.
Use Potato Pete or another vegetable character.

1950s

The 1950s remembered

'Was everything normal again after the war was over?'
Lisa asked her Granny.

'Well no, not immediately, it took a few years before things
returned to normal. Food was still rationed until 1954,
nine years after the end of the war,' Granny said.

'We went down the town to get the messages nearly every day,' Granny continued. 'The grocer's shop wasn't a bit like the modern self-service supermarket. Mr Hughes weighed out tea, sugar, flour, biscuits, and all sorts of things that come in packets now.'

'That must have taken ages,' said Lisa.

'Yes, I suppose it did. But most people didn't mind. There was always someone to talk to, and I didn't have a job outside the home, the way your Mum does,' said Granny.

I remember the first time I saw a banana. I was walking home from school and I saw a boy eating one at his front door. When I got home my mother said she had a big surprise for me. 'Is it a banana?' I exclaimed . . .

19

The grocer's shop

till

weighing scales

shopping basket

delivery bike

KEY ACTIVITIES

Discuss how a grocer's shop in the 1950s differs from
a modern supermarket.

Make a list of some of the things that would have been weighed
out by the grocer in the 1950s that we now buy in packets.
Collect some modern packets of these items.

Why did people in the 1950s need to go to the grocer's shop
nearly every day?

Books and comics

'Have you any books I could read?' Lisa asked Granny.

'I think I might have some of your mother's old annuals,' replied Granny.

'I'd love to see them,' said Lisa.

'I've thrown away most of the old books and comics your mother read. We had lots of them at one time.'

Granny and Lisa climbed up into the roof space to look for old annuals.

Lisa's Granny eventually found some
old books, comics and toys
belonging to the family.

'Oh, I sometimes read *Bunty*,
but Mum's looks very different to mine,'
said Lisa. 'Look, Granny, the
"Four Marys" story is still in my
comic. Imagine, Mum used to
read about them too!'

23

Entertainment

'I remember sitting knitting while your mother and her brothers read their comics. Then at five o'clock we'd all listen to *Children's Hour* on the radio, and we listened to Uncle Mac's *Children's Favourites* on Saturday morning,' recalled Granny. 'Your Mum wrote to Uncle Mac to vote for her favourite record, which was "Nellie the Elephant". My favourite then was "The Runaway Train". I still love to hear it.'

'I never listen to the radio,' said Lisa. 'I'd far rather watch television or play on my computer, and I love going to the pictures.'

'On Saturday afternoon your Mum often went to the cinema. She loved Hopalong Cassidy, Laurel and Hardy, and Roy Rogers. Her favourite film was *King Kong*.'

'Mum still laughs at Laurel and Hardy when we watch them on television,' said Lisa.

'We didn't get a television set until 1959,' Granny said, 'but I remember the first time I saw television. We all went to a neighbour's house to watch the Queen's coronation in 1953, the year your Mum was born. The picture wasn't as good as today's and it was black and white, but we thought it was fantastic.'

25

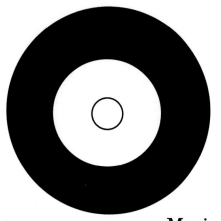

Music

Music and dancing were just as popular in the 1950s as they are today. Young people went to ballrooms and dance halls to jive to local bands like The Royal Showband.

In 1956 everyone began to 'Rock around the Clock' – the new sound of rock-and-roll music. Teddy boys were the height of fashion, with their rubber-soled shoes, colourful socks, 'drainpipe' trousers and long jackets with velvet collars.

record player, 1958

Hits of the 1950s included 'Great Balls of Fire', by Jerry Lee Lewis, 'That'll be the Day', by Buddy Holly and the Crickets, and 'Living Doll', by Cliff Richard. The big American star in those days was Elvis Presley.

KEY ACTIVITIES

Make a list of leisure activities enjoyed at home in the 1950s.
Compare this with things you and your family do in your
spare time. Which of these activities are the same
and which are different?

Design a poster to show what life was like for
young people in the 1950s.

Find pictures of pop stars of the 1950s.
Are any still popular today?
Make a scrapbook with your pictures.

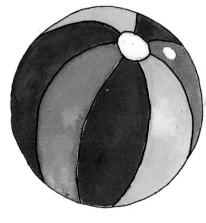

Holidays

Lisa and her Mum were looking at some old holiday snaps one wet afternoon.

'When I was a wee girl we didn't go to Spain and other foreign places on holidays like some people do today,' Mum said.

'Well then, where did you go on holidays, Mum?' asked Lisa.

'I used to love going to the seaside for a day. We usually went to Bangor, Newcastle or Portrush by train,' replied Mum. 'We had a really good time at the amusements and eating candy floss.'

'If we were very lucky we went back to one of those places for a week in the summer,' said Mum, who enjoyed remembering this time in her life.

'When you went away for a week in the summertime, did Grandad take you by car?' asked Lisa.

'Dear me, no. Very few people had cars in those days. Our neighbours had a car and caravan, but that was very unusual,' replied Mum.

29

'The train sounds like more fun than going by car, anyway,' said Lisa, 'so will you take me on a train sometime, Mum?'

'One day this summer we will go on a special steam train journey to Portrush. Wouldn't that be exciting?' replied Mum.

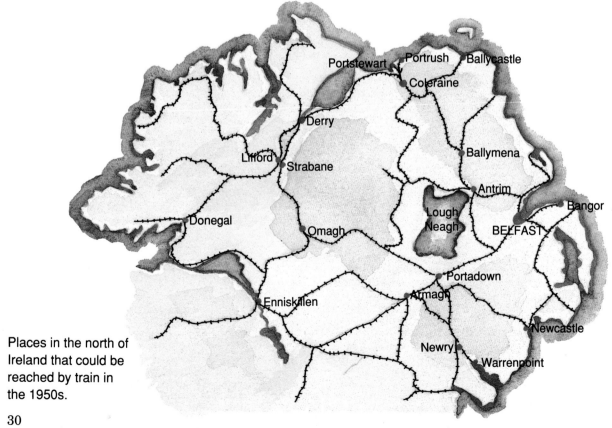

Places in the north of Ireland that could be reached by train in the 1950s.

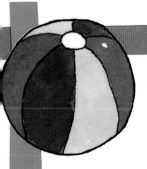

KEY ACTIVITIES

★

Why do you think people went to the seaside for a
day out in the 1950s?
Do you enjoy going to the seaside for a day?

★

Why did fewer people travel to other countries for their
holidays in the 1950s compared with today?

★

Discuss places where people today might spend summer
holidays and the various ways of travelling to those places.

School

'Life at our school was very different to your school today,' Mum told Lisa.

'Tell me about your school, Mum,' replied Lisa. 'It was much smaller than mine, wasn't it?'

A page from a 1950s exercise book

'In our little school in the country,' started Mum, 'we were like one big family.'

Cloy primary school, County Fermanagh, 1956

'The head teacher was known as the Master,' she said, 'and you didn't misbehave too often because you might have been caned.'

'I don't think I would have liked going to your school, Mum,' replied Lisa.

'Oh, we had great fun because our classes were small and we helped to look after the younger chidren,' said Mum. 'We got milk every morning at breaktime, and one of the jobs we had to do was to put straws in the bottles. Another job we liked doing for the teacher was filling the empty ink-wells.'

33

'I remember being caned by the teacher, for dipping my friend's plaits in an ink-well!' Mum giggled.

KEY ACTIVITIES

Ask anyone who went to school in the 1950s to describe
their happiest memories of school.
Make a class scrapbook of these memories.

Make a list of things that have changed and a list of
things that have not changed in schools.

★

Imagine you are in the classroom when someone is cheeky
to the teacher. What do you think might happen?
How would the punishment differ today from what would
have happened in the 1950s?

35

The 1960s remembered

Lisa's Mum works in an office and likes coming home to her bright, modern kitchen. She was a teenager in the 1960s.

'I remember when my Mum first got a twin-tub washing machine. She thought it was wonderful. It was called a twin-tub because it had two tubs, one to wash clothes and one to spin the water out,' she said.

twin-tub washing machine, 1960s

36

electric washing machine
with wringer, 1940s

'Was it as good as ours?' asked Lisa.

'Well, before the twin-tub we had an old machine with a hand wringer on top. So the twin-tub was better than it. But our automatic machine is so much easier to use,' Mum replied. 'I'm very lucky because all I have to do is put the washing in the machine with washing powder, press a button and the machine does the rest. When I was a girl, your Granny spent many more hours cooking and cleaning than we do today.

Modern machines like vacuum cleaners and food processors make housework much easier now than in the past. That's why I have time to take you swimming at the weekends.'

electric refrigerator,
1959

electric cooker,
1935

37

A 1960s kitchen

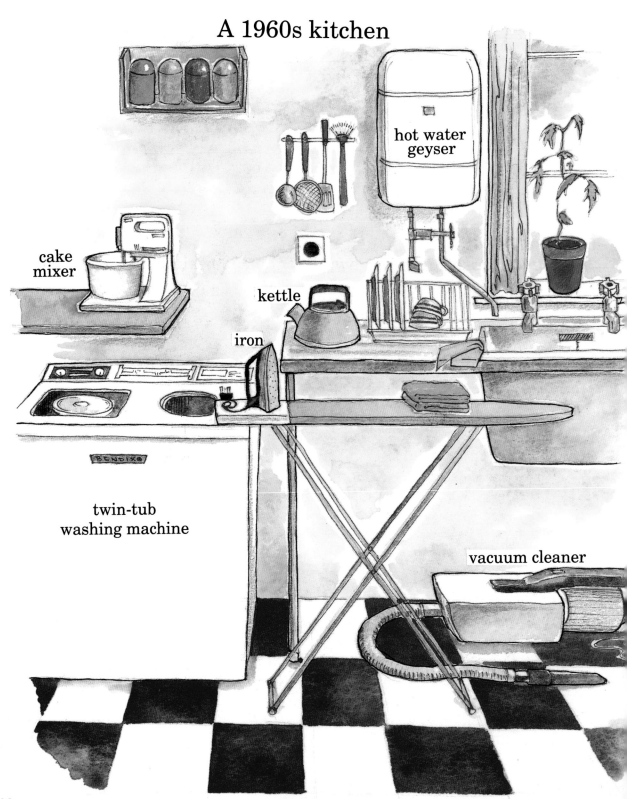

hot water geyser

cake mixer

kettle

iron

twin-tub washing machine

vacuum cleaner

KEY ACTIVITIES

Look closely at the drawing of the 1960s kitchen on page 38.
In what ways is your kitchen similar or different to this one?

Can you think of any new machines that make cooking
and cleaning easier today?

Make a time line to show how the job of washing clothes
has changed.

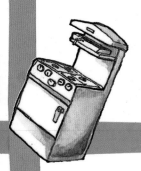

Fashion in the swinging sixties

Clothes changed a lot in the 1960s.

Young people did not want to wear the same kind of clothes as their parents did. Smaller shops called 'boutiques' became very popular with teenagers who wanted to buy the latest fashions. Girls wore short skirts called 'minis', often with 'skinny rib' jumpers and sling back shoes or long boots. Boys wore 'hipster' trousers, and brightly coloured shirts and ties. Coats, boots, and even trousers and skirts, were sometimes made from PVC, a shiny plastic material.

Later in the 1960s the 'hippy' look became popular.
Very long hair became the fashion for young men and
women.

Pop music

Like today, teenagers in the 1960s loved pop music. Small battery-run transistor radios became very popular and young people could now listen to their favourite music programmes even when they were out-of-doors.

Many young people danced the 'Twist' to the music of the American singer Chubby Checker. A British group called The Beatles became the most famous pop group in the world.

The press soon began to talk of Beatlemania as more and more of The Beatles' songs became hits.

© Apple Corps Limited

42

Beatles' fans copied the clothes and hairstyle of the group and thousands went to their concerts. Other famous British groups were The Rolling Stones, The Animals and The Who.

More and more families had their own television sets. Teenagers watched their favourite groups on programmes like *Ready Steady Go* and *Top of the Pops*.

Other popular programmes were *Doctor Who*, *Blue Peter* and *Star Trek*. Younger children enjoyed *Andy Pandy*, *Bill and Ben* and *The Woodentops*.

The Woodentops

Cars

In the early 1960s the Mini motorcar became very popular. This little car cost about £500. Many people, including Lisa's grandparents, bought a Mini as their first car.

'Learning to drive the Mini wasn't difficult,' remembers Granny, 'but you had to push a button on the floor to start the engine after you had switched on the ignition.'

'Were you all able to fit into the Mini?' asked Lisa.

'Oh yes,' replied Grandad, 'and other people had great fun trying to see how many they could squeeze into their Mini.'

1963 Cortina

1969 Capri

1968 Escort

44

KEY ACTIVITIES

Find out about the clothes worn in the 1960s.
Some are in fashion again today.
Why do you think this is so?

Make a list of some pop stars of the 1960s who
are still popular today.

Look for pictures of 1960s cars.
Where might you go to see them?

In 1957 the Soviet Sputnik-2 was launched and a dog called Laika became the first animal in space.

Special world events in the 1960s

The decade of the 1960s was very important for the development of space travel.

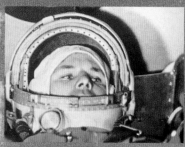

In April 1961 Soviet cosmonaut Yuri Gagarin became the first man to orbit the earth.

In July 1969 American astronaut Neil Armstrong, accompanied by Edwin (Buzz) Aldrin, was the first man to set foot on the moon.

In 1963 Soviet cosmonaut Valentina Tereshkova made a three-day flight in space, becoming the first woman cosmonaut.

Apollo 15 lift off, July 1971, on a lunar landing mission

46

John F. Kennedy, the President of the United States of America, was shot dead in Dallas, Texas, in 1963. This was an important world event which many people remember even today.

The supersonic airliner Concorde made its first test flight in 1969. In the same year British army troops were sent to Northern Ireland when the Troubles started.

Acknowledgements

The authors would like to thank the Belfast Education and Library Board and their families and friends for their help during the preparation of this book.

Grateful acknowledgement is also made to: © Apple Corps Limited, p. 42; Armagh Planetarium, p. 46 and back cover; BBC Enterprises Limited: Harbottle and Lewis, p. 43; Belfast Education and Library Board, p. 4; *Belfast Telegraph* Collection, pp. 40, 47; Blackie and Son Limited, p. 22; British Aerospace Airbus Limited, p. 47; Down County Museum, pp. 26, 37; Charlotte and Joseph Dunbar, p. 36; Dermott Dunbar, pp. 4, 36; Ford Motor Company, p. 44; Hulton-Deutsch Collection Limited, p. 5; *Londonderry Sentinel* Collection, p. 8; Robert Opie Collection, p. 12; Public Record Office, pp. 13, 16; Public Record Office of Northern Ireland, p. 9 and back cover; *Radio Times*, pp. 24, 42, 43; Mary Smyth, pp. 6, 14, 28, 29 and back cover; Richard Smyth, p. 15; D.C. Thomson and Company Limited, pp. 22, 23; © Valentina Tereshkova, p. 46; Sheila Tinsley, p. 12; Ulster Folk and Transport Museum, pp. 10, 11, 32; Sheena Woods, p. 6.

The publishers have made every effort to trace and acknowledge copyright holders. We apologise for any omissions and will welcome additions or amendments for inclusion in any future edition or reprint of this book.

First published in 1994 by
The Blackstaff Press Limited
3 Galway Park, Dundonald, Belfast BT16 0AN, Northern Ireland
with the assistance of
the Department of Education Northern Ireland
Reprinted 1995

© Text, Rhonda Glasgow and Sheila Tinsley, 1994
© Illustrations, Bill Walsh, 1994
All rights reserved

Printed in Singapore by
Toppan Printing Company Limited

A CIP catalogue record for this book
is available from the British Library

ISBN 0-85640-526-4